AMSTERDAM TRAVEL GUIDE 2025

Experience the Best Attractions, Museums, Festivals, Day Trips, Dining and Shopping.

This provides travelers with an in-depth exploration of culture, adventures and hidden spots, providing expert advice, itineraries and essential tips to ensure a memorable and seamless trip.

DANIEL BROWN

All rights reserved. No part of this book may be reproduced, stored in a retrieval system, or transmitted in any form or by any means, electronic, mechanical, photocopying, recording, or otherwise, without the prior written permission of the publisher, except for brief quotations in a book review.

Copyright © 2025 by DANIEL BROWN

TABLE OF CONTENTS

Welcome to Amsterdam 6

A City of Canals and Culture 6

Why Amsterdam is a Must-Visit Destination .. 8

Key Highlights of This Guide 10

Planning Your Adventure 13

Visa and Entry Requirements 13

Navigating Amsterdam 15

Best Time to Visit 18

Currency, Language, and Etiquette Tips 21

Exploring Amsterdam's Neighborhoods. 23

The Iconic Jordaan District 24

De Pijp 26

The Historic Center 29

The Green Haven 32

Unmissable Attractions 35

Anne Frank House 36

Van Gogh Museum............................. 38

The Rijksmuseum 41

Amsterdam's Canals........................... 43

A'DAM Lookout............................... 46

Amsterdam's Cultural Pulse 48

Tulip Mania 49

The Coffee Shop Culture 52

Local Festivals 54

Food and Drink................................. 59

Traditional Dutch Cuisine 59

Where to Find Amsterdam's Best International Cuisine.. 64

Craft Breweries and Distilleries.............67

Top Restaurants and Must-Try Food Tours... 69

Shopping and Souvenirs 72

Unique Finds in Amsterdam's Boutiques and Markets 73

Guide to Local Crafts and Dutch Design 76

Best Spots for Vintage Treasures....................78

Shopping Tips for Souvenirs...........................81

Nightlife and Entertainment................... 83

Amsterdam's Nightlife Scene......................... 84

The Best Theater and Performance Venues ... 89

Unique Experiences 91

Sample Itineraries 95

Amsterdam in 24 Hours 96

Three Days in Amsterdam 100

Family-Friendly Itinerary 105

Day Trips from Amsterdam 110

Zaanse Schans 111

Haarlem...113

Giethoorn 116

Volendam and Edam..........................119

Practical Tips and Resources............... 123

Packing Essentials for Amsterdam...............123

Essential Dutch Phrases for Tourists 126

Emergency Contacts and Safety Tips 128

Insider Hacks to Save Money and Time........ 131

Conclusion.. 134

Welcome to Amsterdam

A City of Canals and Culture

Step into Amsterdam, a city where history and modernity blend seamlessly. Known as the "Venice of the North," Amsterdam enchants visitors with its winding canals, cobblestone streets, and iconic gabled houses. Over 165 canals stretch across the city, creating a picturesque maze that offers not just stunning views but also a unique way of life. These waterways, designated as a UNESCO World Heritage Site, are the veins of Amsterdam's soul—reflecting its history, ingenuity, and charm.

Yet, Amsterdam is far more than its canals. It's a cultural mosaic, teeming with art galleries, historic landmarks, and lively festivals. From the hauntingly powerful Anne Frank House to the exuberant tulip markets, this city invites exploration at every corner. Bicycles whizz by as locals and tourists alike embrace Amsterdam's sustainable lifestyle, while its café culture offers a warm welcome for both relaxed mornings and vibrant evenings.

Amsterdam doesn't just offer sights; it offers experiences that resonate deeply. Picture yourself strolling through the Jordaan District, where narrow streets are lined with art studios and quaint shops. Imagine sipping coffee by a canal, the reflections of 17th-century architecture shimmering in the water. Every moment in Amsterdam feels like stepping into a postcard, one scene more captivating than the next.

Why Amsterdam is a Must-Visit Destination

Why choose Amsterdam for your next adventure? Because it's a city that promises something for everyone. History buffs can delve into the Dutch Golden Age at the Rijksmuseum, art enthusiasts can marvel at Van Gogh's masterpieces, and those seeking a bit of whimsy can immerse themselves in Amsterdam's tulip gardens or its colorful markets.

The city is also a gateway to Dutch innovation and inclusivity. Known for its progressive values, Amsterdam has long been a pioneer in sustainability, diversity, and creative freedom. It's a city that welcomes all, from solo adventurers to families with kids, from backpackers to luxury travelers.

Food lovers will rejoice at Amsterdam's culinary offerings. Whether you're sampling traditional Dutch dishes like bitterballen or indulging in international cuisines from the city's diverse immigrant communities, your taste buds are in for a treat. And let's not forget the beer—Amsterdam's craft breweries and traditional pubs are an experience in themselves.

Beyond the surface, Amsterdam is a city that tells stories. It's the story of resilience, as reflected in its recovery from floods and war. It's the story of innovation, seen in its futuristic sustainability initiatives. And it's the story of connection, where locals and visitors alike share in the joys of its festivals, nightlife, and everyday rhythms.

Key Highlights of This Guide

This guide is your ultimate companion to discovering Amsterdam in 2025. Packed with up-to-date information and local insights, it's designed to help you unlock the city's magic, whether you're visiting for the first time or returning to uncover new treasures. Here's what you can look forward to:

- **Comprehensive Travel Tips:** From navigating the city's famous bike culture to understanding its public transport system, you'll learn how to get around like a pro.

- **Insider Recommendations:** Discover hidden gems that only locals know, from tucked-away cafés to secret gardens.

- **Curated Itineraries:** No matter how much time you have—24 hours, three days, or a week—our itineraries ensure you experience the best of Amsterdam.

- **Unmissable Attractions:** Learn about Amsterdam's must-see sights, including the Anne Frank House, the Van Gogh Museum, and its iconic canal cruises.

- **Cultural Immersion:** Gain a deeper understanding of Amsterdam's traditions, festivals, and unique way of life.

- **Food and Drink Adventures:** Find out where to savor the best Dutch delicacies and explore the city's vibrant dining scene.

- **Day Trips and Beyond:** Extend your trip with day trips to nearby towns, each offering its own charm and character.

Whether you're drawn to Amsterdam's history, art, or laid-back vibe, this guide is here to make your visit unforgettable. More than just a travel book, it's an invitation to see Amsterdam through the eyes of those who know it best.

Planning Your Adventure

Planning a trip to Amsterdam is like preparing for a journey into a world of charm, culture, and unforgettable experiences. To make the most of your adventure, you'll need a blend of practical preparation and a curiosity for discovery.

Visa and Entry Requirements

Amsterdam, as part of the Netherlands, is in the Schengen Area, which simplifies travel for many visitors.

- **Schengen Visa Requirements**: If you're a citizen of a country that requires a

Schengen visa, ensure you apply well in advance. You'll need valid travel insurance, proof of accommodation, a return ticket, and sufficient funds for your stay. The visa usually allows access to 26 European countries, making it an excellent option if you plan to explore beyond Amsterdam.

- Visa-Free Entry: Travelers from many countries, including the US, UK, Australia, Canada, and New Zealand, can visit for up to 90 days without a visa. However, starting in 2025, you may need an **ETIAS (European Travel Information and Authorization System)** authorization, so check requirements before booking.

- Border Control Tips: Keep your passport or ID handy and ensure it's valid for at least six months beyond your travel dates. A warm smile and clear answers about your trip plans will help you breeze through customs.

Navigating Amsterdam
Public Transport and Bike Culture

Amsterdam is a city that thrives on seamless mobility, making it easy for visitors to get around. The two cornerstones of transportation here are an efficient public transport network and an unparalleled bike culture.

- **Public Transport:** Amsterdam boasts an excellent transport system operated by **GVB**, including trams, buses, metro lines, and ferries.

    - **Trams:** The lifeblood of the city, trams are quick and reliable for short distances. Major tourist spots are well connected.

- Metro: Perfect for reaching areas outside the city center, such as Amsterdam-Noord.

- Buses: Convenient for routes where trams don't operate, including late-night options.

- Ferries: Free ferries from Central Station to Amsterdam-Noord provide a unique perspective of the city from the water.

- Tickets and Apps: The OV-chipkaart is your best friend for travel. Load it with credit and enjoy hassle-free transport. Alternatively, purchase daily or multi-day passes for unlimited rides. GVB's app offers real-time updates and route planning.

- **The Bike Culture**: Amsterdam is synonymous with bicycles. Over 800,000 bikes traverse its streets daily. Renting a bike is one of the best ways to explore the city like a local.

  - **Bike Rentals**: Many shops near Central Station and key areas offer rentals, with prices typically starting at €10 per day.

  - **Cycling Rules**: Stick to designated bike lanes, always use hand signals, and be mindful of pedestrians and trams.

  - **Cycling Tips**: Start with less crowded areas like Vondelpark before venturing into busier streets. Helmets are optional but recommended.

Navigating Amsterdam is an experience in itself, whether you're hopping on a tram, pedaling through its lanes, or gliding across the canals on a ferry.

Best Time to Visit
Seasons and Festivals

Amsterdam is beautiful year-round, but the vibe of the city changes dramatically with the seasons. Here's what you can expect:

- **Spring (March to May)**:

    - Famous for its tulips, spring is a magical time. The Keukenhof Gardens are in full bloom, and the annual **Tulip Festival** paints the city in vibrant colors.

    - Temperatures range from 6–15°C (43–59°F), so bring layers.

    - Don't miss **King's Day (April 27)**, a nationwide celebration where the city turns orange and streets overflow with music, markets, and joy.

- **Summer (June to August)**:

  - The city is alive with festivals, outdoor events, and sunny days. Canals brim with boats, and parks like Vondelpark are buzzing with activity.

  - Average temperatures hover around 20°C (68°F), perfect for exploring.

  - Events like **Pride Amsterdam** in August showcase the city's inclusivity and creativity.

- **Autumn (September to November)**:

  - Crisp air and golden leaves make this a romantic time to visit. The **Amsterdam Dance Event** draws music lovers from around the globe.

- Temperatures range from 5–15°C (41–59°F), so pack a warm coat.

- **Winter (December to February)**:

  - Amsterdam transforms into a winter wonderland with twinkling lights and cozy cafés. The **Amsterdam Light Festival** illuminates the city, while Christmas markets add festive charm.

  - Temperatures can drop to 0°C (32°F), so bundle up.

  - Ice skating on the canals (if frozen) is a magical experience.

Each season offers unique opportunities to fall in love with Amsterdam, making it a destination you'll want to revisit.

Currency, Language, and Etiquette Tips

Understanding the local nuances will help you feel right at home.

- **Currency:**

    o Amsterdam uses the **Euro (€)**. Credit and debit cards are widely accepted, but cash is still handy for small transactions.

    o ATMs are plentiful, and most support international cards. Look for those marked with "Geldmaat."

    o Tipping is appreciated but not obligatory. Rounding up the bill or leaving 5-10% at restaurants is customary.

- **Language:**

    o The official language is Dutch, but nearly everyone speaks English fluently. Don't hesitate to ask for help; locals are friendly and accommodating.

- Learning a few Dutch phrases can enhance your experience. Start with basics like:

  - Hallo! (Hello)

  - Dank je wel! (Thank you)

  - *Alsjeblieft* (Please/Here you go)

- Etiquette:

  - Punctuality is valued, so arrive on time for tours or appointments.

  - Respect bike lanes—they're sacred to locals!

  - At cafés and restaurants, it's common to wait for the server to bring the bill rather than asking immediately.

Exploring Amsterdam's Neighborhoods

Amsterdam is a city of distinct neighborhoods, each with its own personality, charm, and hidden gems. The beauty of Amsterdam lies in its diversity, and the best way to experience it is by wandering through its unique districts. Whether you're looking for artistic vibes, vibrant food scenes, or quiet canal-side strolls, there's a neighborhood that matches every traveler's desire.

The Iconic Jordaan District
Art, Cafés, and Charm

Nestled in the heart of Amsterdam, the Jordaan is undoubtedly one of the most charming and picturesque neighborhoods in the city. Known for its narrow, cobblestone streets and stunning canal-side houses, the Jordaan captures the essence of old-world Amsterdam while blending in a modern artistic edge. It's a place where you can get lost in the beauty of the canals, discover hidden courtyards, and enjoy a local experience that feels far removed from the typical tourist trail.

1. A Creative Hub:

The Jordaan is a haven for artists, creatives, and those with an appreciation for design. Once a working-class neighborhood, it has evolved into one of the city's most sought-after areas, with art galleries, independent shops, and vintage boutiques lining the streets. For art lovers, the area is dotted with contemporary galleries showcasing both local and international artists. Whether it's a traditional Dutch landscape or a quirky modern piece, the Jordaan's art scene will captivate you.

2. Cafés and Local Delights:

One of the joys of exploring the Jordaan is its vibrant café culture. Imagine sipping coffee in an intimate café, surrounded by beautiful canal views. Many of the cafés in the Jordaan have an old-world feel, with cozy interiors and a relaxed atmosphere. You'll find a mix of traditional Dutch cafés and trendy spots serving up artisanal pastries, gourmet coffee, and inventive dishes. Be sure to stop by Café

Winkel 43, home to arguably the best Dutch apple pie in Amsterdam.

3. Must-Visit Landmarks:

Anne Frank House: A poignant and significant site, this museum is located in the heart of the Jordaan and offers a glimpse into the life of Anne Frank and the Holocaust.

Noorderkerk: A beautiful 17th-century church that serves as a focal point for the Jordaan's community.

Westermarkt: A lively square at the edge of the Jordaan with markets, shops, and restaurants, providing a perfect ending to your stroll.

De Pijp

If you're after a lively, multicultural atmosphere with a touch of bohemian charm, then De Pijp is the neighborhood for you. Just south of the city center, De Pijp is one of Amsterdam's most vibrant districts, known for its diverse population, eclectic mix of restaurants, and boho vibes. This area has evolved over the years, becoming a popular destination for young locals and international travelers.

1. A Culinary Wonderland:

De Pijp is a food lover's paradise, offering an array of dining options that reflect the multicultural makeup of the neighborhood. From Turkish and Moroccan eateries to Thai street food stalls, you can taste your way around the world here. A visit to the famous Albert Cuyp Market is a must—it's one of the largest and oldest street markets in the city. Whether you're looking to sample Dutch herring, buy fresh produce, or grab a quick snack, the market is a bustling hub of activity.

2. Trendy Boutiques and Coffee Shops:

De Pijp is home to some of the coolest boutiques, vintage stores, and artisanal shops. You can easily spend hours wandering through the streets, stopping by independent stores for unique clothing, quirky souvenirs, and local products. The neighborhood also has a thriving café culture, with an abundance of hip coffee shops offering locally roasted beans and Instagram-worthy interiors.

3. A Relaxed Vibe:

Despite its liveliness, De Pijp has a relaxed and laid-back atmosphere. It's an ideal place to unwind, whether you're enjoying a meal at one of the many outdoor cafés or spending a lazy afternoon at Sarphatipark, a tranquil green space in the heart of the neighborhood.

The Historic Center
Dam Square and Beyond

Amsterdam's historic center is the beating heart of the city, and it's here that you'll find the majority of Amsterdam's most famous landmarks, museums, and attractions. This area is a blend of historic buildings, bustling squares, and tourist hubs, making it the perfect spot to begin your exploration of the city.

1. Dam Square: The City's Hub:

At the center of it all is Dam Square, one of Amsterdam's most famous public spaces. Surrounded by iconic buildings such as the Royal Palace, National Monument, and Nieuwe Kerk, Dam Square is a bustling hub where you can find street performers, local vendors, and tourists from around the world. It's a lively spot for people-watching and soaking up the city's vibrant energy.

2. The Royal Palace and Beyond:

A short stroll from Dam Square takes you to some of Amsterdam's most celebrated museums, including the Rijksmuseum, home to masterpieces by Rembrandt and Vermeer, and the Van Gogh Museum, which houses the largest collection of Van Gogh's work in the world. Just down the road, Rembrandtplein offers more art, culture, and great spots for dinner and drinks.

3. Canal-side Charm and Shopping:

The historic center is also a shopper's paradise, with a mix of high-end boutiques, department stores, and charming shops along the Nine Streets (De Negen Straatjes). After indulging in a bit of retail therapy, take a leisurely stroll along the canals or hop on a canal boat to see the city from a different perspective.

The Green Haven

Amsterdam-Noord and Its Hidden Gems

Amsterdam-Noord, located across the IJ River from the city center, is one of the city's most up-and-coming districts, offering a refreshing contrast to the more tourist-heavy areas. While this part of Amsterdam may not have the same historical significance as other neighborhoods, it has quickly become a hotspot for creatives, locals, and travelers looking for a more authentic experience.

1. A Modern, Artsy District:

Amsterdam-Noord is home to cutting-edge architecture, trendy bars, and independent art spaces. The area is filled with converted industrial buildings, many of which now host galleries, co-working spaces, and hip cafés. A visit to the NDSM Werf, an old shipyard turned cultural hub, is a must. This sprawling area is filled with street art, sculpture parks, and quirky installations.

2. A Scenic Escape:

Despite its industrial past, Amsterdam-Noord offers beautiful natural spaces and peaceful, green surroundings. The Noorderpark is perfect for a leisurely afternoon walk or picnic. For those who enjoy more unique experiences, take the free ferry across the IJ River, which not only connects the district to the city center but also offers stunning views of Amsterdam's skyline.

3. Off the Beaten Path:

Though Amsterdam-Noord is increasingly becoming a popular spot for tourists, it still feels off the beaten path. It's an excellent place for travelers who want to experience a more local side of Amsterdam while being just a short ferry ride away from the city center. Here, you'll find fantastic restaurants serving fresh, local food, craft breweries, and a creative, youthful atmosphere.

Unmissable Attractions

Amsterdam is a city that seamlessly blends rich history, world-class art, and modern attractions. Whether you're a history buff, an art lover, or simply someone who enjoys a stunning view, Amsterdam has something extraordinary to offer. This section will guide you through some of the city's most unmissable attractions—each one providing a unique glimpse into the soul of Amsterdam.

Anne Frank House
A Testament to History

Among the most poignant and emotionally charged sites in Amsterdam, the Anne Frank House stands as a testament to the resilience of the human spirit. Located in the heart of the Jordaan district, this museum occupies the actual building where Anne Frank and her family hid during the Nazi occupation of the Netherlands.

1. A Historical Pilgrimage:

Visiting the Anne Frank House is a deeply moving experience. As you step inside, you're taken back in time to the cramped rooms where Anne Frank wrote her famous diary. The secret annex, which was concealed behind a bookshelf, provides a haunting reminder of the harsh realities of war and persecution. The museum not only tells Anne's story but also paints a broader picture of the Jewish community's experiences during the Holocaust.

2. The Diary of Anne Frank:

Anne's diary is the heart and soul of the museum. The museum features passages from her diary, alongside photographs and personal artifacts, offering insight into her thoughts and dreams. Anne's writing, which has touched millions worldwide, continues to resonate, and the museum serves as a place for reflection on human rights, tolerance, and the consequences of prejudice.

3. The Experience:

Visitors are encouraged to walk through the rooms as they were during Anne's time. The atmosphere is somber yet empowering, allowing visitors to reflect on the enduring relevance of Anne's words. It's recommended to book tickets in advance, as the museum can get very busy, particularly during peak travel seasons.

Van Gogh Museum
A Journey Through Art

For art lovers, a trip to the Van Gogh Museum is a must. Dedicated to the life and work of Vincent van Gogh, the museum houses the largest collection of his paintings and drawings in the world. From his early works in the Netherlands to the iconic paintings created in France, Van Gogh's artistic journey is brought to life in stunning detail.

1. The Life of a Genius:

The Van Gogh Museum isn't just about admiring the beauty of Van Gogh's art; it's also a profound journey into the mind of one of the most celebrated—and misunderstood—artists of all time. The museum traces his development from his early, darker works to his later masterpieces, such as Sunflowers, The Bedroom, and Starry Night Over the Rhone.

2. More Than Just Paintings:

The museum features more than 200 paintings, along with 500 drawings and over 700 letters that offer an intimate look at Van Gogh's personal struggles, his relationships, and his intense passion for painting. The emotional intensity of his work, combined with his innovative techniques, has made Van Gogh one of the most influential figures in the art world.

3. Temporary Exhibitions and Special Events:

The Van Gogh Museum also hosts rotating exhibitions, providing additional context to the artist's work. Whether showcasing his contemporaries or exploring the broader movement of post-impressionism, these exhibitions add an extra layer of depth to your experience.

The Rijksmuseum
Dutch Masterpieces Unveiled

When it comes to museums, the Rijksmuseum is in a league of its own. As one of the most renowned museums in the world, the Rijksmuseum offers an extraordinary collection of Dutch masterpieces, some of which define the country's cultural heritage. It's the ideal place to immerse yourself in Dutch history, art, and culture.

1. A World-Class Collection:

The Rijksmuseum is home to over 8,000 objects, ranging from medieval armor to Golden Age paintings. Its most famous collection is undoubtedly the works from the Dutch Golden Age, including masterpieces by Rembrandt, Vermeer, and Frans Hals. The highlight, of course, is Rembrandt's The Night Watch, which captivates visitors with its grandeur and historical significance.

Amsterdam Travel Guide 2025

2. The Dutch Golden Age:

The museum offers a rich exploration of the 17th century, a period when the Netherlands was a world power. Paintings by Johannes Vermeer, including The Milkmaid, are some of the most beloved works in the collection. The Rijksmuseum provides context for this period in Dutch history, allowing visitors to appreciate the cultural and political climate in which these masterpieces were created.

3. A Stunning Building:

The Rijksmuseum itself is a work of art. The building, designed by architect Pierre Cuypers, is a stunning example of neo-Gothic architecture. It's not only a place to explore world-class art but also a gorgeous building to admire. After a renovation in recent years, the museum has reopened with even more emphasis on accessibility and visitor experience.

Amsterdam's Canals
UNESCO World Heritage at Its Best

One of Amsterdam's most iconic features is its intricate network of canals, which have shaped the city's identity for centuries. The Canal Ring, or Grachtengordel, is a UNESCO World Heritage site, recognized for its historical significance, beauty, and engineering marvel.

1. The Heart of Amsterdam:

The canals are an essential part of Amsterdam's urban landscape. The Canal Ring, with its concentric circles, was constructed in the 17th century during the Dutch Golden Age and was designed to facilitate trade and transport. Today, the canals are not only functional but also form some of the city's most scenic spots.

2. Canal Cruises:

One of the best ways to see the city is by boat. Canal cruises provide a unique perspective of Amsterdam, with the city's charming houses, bridges, and cobbled streets visible from the water. You can choose from a variety of tours, including private boat rentals, evening cruises, or even dinner cruises, each offering a different experience of the city.

3. Walking Along the Canals:

If you prefer to stay on land, a leisurely walk along the canals is equally rewarding. Stroll past the canal houses, stop for a coffee at one of the many waterside cafés, or explore the quaint shops and boutiques along the way. The canals provide an atmospheric setting for a day of sightseeing, shopping, or simply relaxing.

A'DAM Lookout

Views That Take Your Breath Away

For a view of Amsterdam that's truly unforgettable, head to A'DAM Lookout, an observation deck located across the IJ River in Amsterdam-Noord. Offering panoramic views of the city, the Lookout is the perfect spot to take in the stunning landscape of Amsterdam's historic center, canals, and beyond.

1. The View:

At 100 meters high, A'DAM Lookout provides breathtaking views of the city, from the iconic canal belt to the lush greenery of Amsterdam-Noord. You'll see the historic center in all its glory, with its distinctive rooftops, winding canals, and landmark buildings.

2. Thrill-Seeker's Delight:

For those looking for an extra thrill, A'DAM Lookout features "Over the Edge", Europe's highest swing, where you can swing 100 meters above the ground, overlooking the city. It's an exhilarating experience that offers a new perspective on Amsterdam.

3. Dining and Relaxing:

At the top of the tower, you'll find a restaurant and bar offering drinks and meals with a view. Whether you're sipping a cocktail as the sun sets or enjoying a meal while looking over the city, it's a perfect way to unwind after a day of exploring.

Amsterdam's Cultural Pulse

Amsterdam isn't just a city—it's a living, breathing canvas where tradition and modernity collide in the most unexpected yet delightful ways. From its vibrant tulip fields to its unique coffee shop culture and lively festivals, Amsterdam pulses with energy, creativity, and a deep sense of identity. Whether you're strolling along flower-lined streets, sipping on a coffee at a local café, or dancing in the streets during a festival, the cultural heart of Amsterdam is always beating.

Tulip Mania
Bloemenmarkt and the Keukenhof Gardens

If there's one thing Amsterdam is globally known for, it's its tulips. These vibrant, colorful flowers have a historical significance that goes beyond simple decoration. The story of Tulip Mania, one of the most fascinating periods in Dutch history, has put Amsterdam at the heart of flower culture worldwide.

1. The History of Tulip Mania:

Tulips were introduced to the Netherlands in the 16th century, and by the 17th century, they had become a symbol of wealth and prestige. The infamous Tulip Mania reached its peak between 1634 and 1637, when the price of a single tulip bulb soared to astronomical heights—some bulbs were traded for more than the cost of a house! While the tulip bubble eventually burst, the flowers have remained a cultural cornerstone of the Netherlands. Today, tulips symbolize the nation's beauty, resilience, and creativity.

2. Bloemenmarkt: A Floating Flower Market:

One of the best places to experience Amsterdam's tulip culture is at the Bloemenmarkt, the world's only floating flower market. Located along the Singel Canal, the Bloemenmarkt is a vibrant market filled with flowers, plants, and gardening supplies. While it's a great spot to pick up fresh tulips or souvenirs like tulip-themed bulbs and trinkets, it's also a place to immerse yourself in the heart of Amsterdam's floral heritage. The market has been a part of the city since the 19th century and remains a beloved local and tourist attraction.

3. Keukenhof Gardens: A Feast for the Eyes:

For the ultimate tulip experience, a visit to Keukenhof Gardens, just outside Amsterdam, is a must. Known as the Garden of Europe, Keukenhof is the largest flower garden in the world, covering 79 acres. It is home to millions of tulips, as well as other flowers such as daffodils, hyacinths, and lilies. During the spring months, the garden bursts into a kaleidoscope of colors, drawing visitors from all over the globe. It's a photographer's paradise and a tranquil place to soak in the beauty of Dutch horticultural prowess.

The Coffee Shop Culture
A Unique Amsterdam Experience

Amsterdam is renowned for its unique coffee shop culture—an aspect of the city that sets it apart from other global metropolises. But these are not your typical cafés. Coffee shops in Amsterdam have a special place in the city's social landscape, offering a relaxed, open-minded atmosphere that aligns with the city's progressive and liberal ideals.

1. What's a Coffee Shop?

In Amsterdam, the term "coffee shop" refers to a café where cannabis can be legally purchased and consumed. While the sale and use of cannabis are officially tolerated in the city, it remains illegal in the broader Netherlands. However, in Amsterdam, these establishments offer a safe, regulated environment for people to enjoy cannabis in a responsible manner. Visitors from all over the world come to experience this aspect of Dutch culture—it's a facet of the city that can be both fascinating and fun.

2. A Chill Environment:

The vibe in Amsterdam's coffee shops is typically laid-back and inclusive. These spaces often feature comfortable seating, soft music, and friendly staff who are happy to help customers navigate the menu of cannabis strains, edibles, and drinks. While the most famous coffee shops, like The Bulldog and Coffeeshop Amsterdam, are well-known, many locals prefer the quieter, less tourist-heavy spots. Coffee shops are an essential part of the city's countercultural scene and offer visitors a glimpse into the city's progressive values of freedom and tolerance.

3. Etiquette in the Coffee Shops:

If you plan to visit a coffee shop, there are a few things to keep in mind. While the atmosphere is relaxed, it's essential to be respectful of others and mindful of your surroundings. It's also important to remember that alcohol is not allowed in coffee shops, and consumption is strictly regulated. If you're not familiar with cannabis, it's a good idea to ask the staff for recommendations or start with small quantities, as the potency of cannabis products can vary.

Local Festivals
King's Day, Amsterdam Pride, and More

Amsterdam is a city that knows how to throw a good party. From vibrant national celebrations to colorful international events, the city's festival calendar is packed year-round, offering something for everyone. These festivals are a reflection of Amsterdam's diverse, open-minded, and celebratory spirit. Let's explore three of the most iconic celebrations that capture the essence of Amsterdam's cultural vibrancy.

1. King's Day (Koningsdag): A National Celebration Like No Other

King's Day, celebrated every April 27th, is the Netherlands' most significant national holiday. On this day, Amsterdam transforms into a sea of orange, as people dress in orange attire (the Dutch royal color) to celebrate the King's birthday. The streets are filled with music, street markets, and vibrant parties, creating a fun, carefree atmosphere that's contagious.

- The Streets Are Alive:

The entire city becomes one big street party. The canals are packed with boats, some decked out with speakers and DJs, while others host impromptu performances and parties. Street vendors sell everything from food to second-hand goods in a massive flea market known as Vrijmarkt.

- The Energy:

The energy is electrifying, and it's impossible not to get swept up in the excitement. Locals and tourists alike come together to celebrate, enjoying the sense of unity and joy that fills the air. It's one of the best times to experience the warmth and friendliness of the Dutch people.

2. Amsterdam Pride: A Celebration of Love and Equality

Amsterdam Pride, typically held in August, is one of the largest LGBTQ+ celebrations in the world. The festival spans several days, but the highlight is the iconic Canal Parade, where elaborately decorated boats filled with LGBTQ+ activists, artists, and allies sail along the canals in a powerful display of love, acceptance, and equality.

- A Colorful, Inclusive Event:

Pride in Amsterdam is a celebration of diversity, and it attracts millions of visitors who come to show their support for the LGBTQ+ community. The event is marked by inclusive parties, cultural exhibitions, and performances, creating an atmosphere of freedom and creativity.

- More Than Just a Parade:

Amsterdam Pride is more than just a parade—it's a platform for discussing social issues, fighting for equal rights, and celebrating love in all its forms. The festival encourages everyone to express themselves authentically, regardless of their identity or background.

3. Other Notable Festivals:

While King's Day and Amsterdam Pride are the most iconic, Amsterdam hosts a variety of other festivals that highlight its diverse cultural offerings. The Amsterdam Light Festival (held in winter) transforms the city into a glowing wonderland, with light installations and art projects adorning the canals. The Amsterdam Dance Event (ADE) brings together electronic music lovers from around the world for an unparalleled party experience. Additionally, The Holland Festival celebrates theater, dance, and music from both local and international artists, making it a cultural highlight of the summer.

Food and Drink

Amsterdam is not just a feast for the eyes with its picturesque canals, historic neighborhoods, and world-class art—it's also a city that will delight your taste buds. From traditional Dutch comfort food to a global fusion of international flavors, the city offers a culinary experience that is as rich and diverse as its culture. Whether you're nibbling on a stroopwafel by the canal, savoring herring from a street stall, or sipping a local craft beer, Amsterdam's food and drink scene will take you on a journey that engages all your senses.

Traditional Dutch Cuisine
Stroopwafels, Herring, and Bitterballen

When you think of Dutch cuisine, you might not immediately imagine a vibrant culinary scene, but the Netherlands has a few key dishes that have stood the test of time. These traditional foods are simple yet hearty and are an essential part of the Amsterdam experience.

1. Stroopwafels: A Sweet, Heavenly Treat

One of the most iconic Dutch snacks, the stroopwafel (literally "syrup waffle") is a sweet, warm treat that has become a beloved part of Dutch culture. Made by sandwiching a layer of caramel syrup between two thin, crispy waffles, this gooey delicacy is often enjoyed with a cup of coffee or tea. While it can be found in supermarkets and markets throughout Amsterdam, the best way to enjoy it is at one of the street vendors or at the Albert Cuyp Market, where you can buy a freshly made stroopwafel that's warm, gooey, and utterly irresistible.

2. Herring: A Bold Dutch Delicacy

Amsterdam is a city by the water, so it's no surprise that seafood plays a major role in the city's food culture. One of the most famous Dutch dishes is raw herring, or haring. Served with finely chopped onions and pickles, herring is traditionally eaten by holding the fish by its tail and taking a bite, though many prefer to eat it with a fork. It's a simple, briny treat that is beloved by locals, and a visit to Amsterdam wouldn't be complete without sampling it from a herring stand. For the most authentic experience, try it at Haringhandel in the heart of the city, a small stall that has been serving fresh herring for generations.

3. Bitterballen: A Perfect Pub Snack

When it comes to traditional Dutch comfort food, bitterballen reigns supreme. These savory deep-fried balls of beef ragout are crunchy on the outside and creamy on the inside, making them the perfect snack to enjoy with a cold beer. Often served with mustard for dipping, they are a popular choice at bars, pubs, and cafés around the city. You'll find bitterballen on almost every menu in Amsterdam, but a great place to try them is Café 't Smalle, a cozy spot in the Jordaan district known for its excellent Dutch snacks and hearty local brews.

Where to Find Amsterdam's Best International Cuisine

While traditional Dutch food has its charm, Amsterdam is a city that embraces culinary diversity. Thanks to its international population and vibrant food scene, the city offers an incredible array of global cuisines. Whether you're craving Italian, Middle Eastern, Asian, or Caribbean food, you'll find it all in Amsterdam's eclectic neighborhoods.

1. The Food Scene in De Pijp: A Melting Pot of Global Flavors

De Pijp is one of Amsterdam's most culturally diverse neighborhoods, and its food scene reflects this. The area is home to a variety of ethnic restaurants that serve up delicious and authentic dishes from around the world. From Turkish kebabs and Middle Eastern mezze to Indonesian rijsttafel (a traditional Dutch colonial dish with a variety of small dishes), De Pijp has it all. Be sure to visit The Seafood Bar for fresh seafood or Bazar, a vibrant restaurant with a colorful interior offering dishes inspired by North African and Middle Eastern flavors.

2. Chinatown and Indonesian Influence

Amsterdam's Chinatown, located near the Central Station, is the place to go for Chinese, Thai, and Malaysian cuisine. The Chinese supermarkets and eateries here offer a chance to sample some of the best dim sum, noodles, and rice dishes in the city. Don't miss out on the famous Indonesian rijsttafel, a feast of rice accompanied by numerous small side dishes. Many of the best Indonesian restaurants can be found near the city's central area, including Kantjil & de Tijger and Sampurna—both are popular for their flavorful and diverse spreads.

3. Italian Excellence in the City

If you're craving a taste of Italy, Amsterdam's Italian restaurants are the next best thing to dining in Rome or Florence. Casa di David, located in the city center, is a sophisticated yet relaxed spot offering authentic pasta, risotto, and pizza. For a more casual but equally delicious experience, head to La Perla in the Jordaan for fresh pizza made with high-quality ingredients and a crust that's crispy and perfect every time.

Craft Breweries and Distilleries
Tasting Local Beers and Jenever

Amsterdam's craft beer scene has exploded in recent years, with local breweries popping up all over the city. Whether you're a beer connoisseur or a casual drinker, Amsterdam offers some unique flavors that you won't find anywhere else.

1. Craft Breweries:

The Netherlands has a long-standing tradition of brewing, and Amsterdam has embraced the craft beer revolution with enthusiasm. Local breweries like Brouwerij 't IJ, located in a windmill near the Amstel River, offer a variety of beers brewed with unique flavors inspired by the city's history and culture. Other notable breweries include De Prael, which produces a range of craft beers with a focus on quality and sustainability, and Oedipus Brewing, known for its bold and experimental brews. Many of these breweries offer tours and tastings, allowing you to learn about the brewing process while sampling some delicious beers.

2. Jenever: A Dutch Spirit Worth Sipping

Jenever, often referred to as Dutch gin, is a spirit that has been produced in the Netherlands for centuries. Unlike gin, which is often flavored with juniper berries, jenever is made from malt wine and is typically served as a neat shot in Amsterdam's traditional bars. To truly experience jenever, head to one of the city's historic brown cafés (traditional Dutch pubs), such as Proeflokaal Arendsnest. Here, you can try a wide variety of jenever, from classic flavors to innovative new blends. For a deeper dive into the history of this beloved spirit, consider a tour at The House of Bols Cocktail & Genever Experience, where you can learn about the distillation process and enjoy tastings of both jenever and expertly crafted cocktails.

Top Restaurants and Must-Try Food Tours

Amsterdam is a foodie's paradise, with a broad selection of restaurants that cater to all tastes and budgets. Here are some of the city's top restaurants and must-try food tours that will make your trip unforgettable:

1. De Silveren Spiegel

This elegant Dutch restaurant, located in a historic 16th-century building, is perfect for experiencing classic Dutch cuisine with a modern twist. Their menu changes seasonally, but dishes like stamppot (mashed potatoes with vegetables and sausage) are a must-try.

2. The Pancake Bakery

For a true Dutch breakfast experience, visit The Pancake Bakery, where you can enjoy giant pancakes filled with a variety of toppings—both savory and sweet.

3. Moeders

A cozy restaurant that celebrates Dutch home-cooking, Moeders serves up hearty, comforting dishes like hutspot (a stew made with potatoes, carrots, and onions). The walls are decorated with photos of mothers from around the world, making it feel like home.

4. Food Tours in Amsterdam

For those wanting to get a deeper taste of the city's food scene, a food tour is the best way to explore Amsterdam's culinary diversity. Tours like Amsterdam Food Tours offer a guided walk through neighborhoods like the Jordaan or De Pijp, where you can sample everything from street food to artisanal treats. The Dutch Food Adventure tour takes you through Amsterdam's best food markets, giving you the chance to taste Dutch specialties like cheese, sausages, and freshly baked pastries.

5. Vlaamsch Broodhuys

For artisanal breads, cakes, and pastries, Vlaamsch Broodhuys is a must-visit. Their selection of freshly baked goods is perfect for breakfast or an afternoon snack.

Shopping and Souvenirs

Amsterdam is not only a city rich in culture and history but also a vibrant shopping destination with a diverse selection of boutiques, markets, and quirky shops. Whether you're hunting for unique souvenirs to take home, indulging in high-end fashion, or seeking out hidden treasures, Amsterdam offers an exceptional retail experience. From luxurious design stores to bustling flea markets, the city caters to every kind of shopper, making it an ideal destination for those looking to bring a piece of the Netherlands home with them.

Unique Finds in Amsterdam's Boutiques and Markets

Amsterdam's shopping scene is anything but predictable. If you're looking for something truly unique, the city's boutiques, independent stores, and famous markets are the places to visit. Here, you'll find everything from one-of-a-kind fashion items to locally crafted goods that you can't get anywhere else.

1. The Nine Streets (De Negen Straatjes)

If you want to shop in a neighborhood full of charming boutiques, then head straight to De Negen Straatjes (The Nine Streets), a picturesque area nestled between the city's famous canals. This charming shopping district is filled with independent shops offering a range of unique finds—from custom-made leather goods and high-end fashion to quirky jewelry and vintage items. Walk down these cobblestone streets, and you'll find small stores that are perfect for finding something special to bring home. One such gem is The Greenhouse, a boutique that offers eco-friendly fashion and accessories, perfect for those looking to support sustainable brands.

2. Amsterdam's Famous Markets: Albert Cuyp and Noordermarkt

For an authentic Amsterdam shopping experience, a visit to one of the city's famous markets is a must. The Albert Cuyp Market in De Pijp is Amsterdam's largest and most famous street market. Here, you'll find an eclectic mix of stalls selling everything from fresh produce and cheese to Dutch antiques and handmade jewelry. It's a great place to pick up unique souvenirs, especially if you're after local products like Dutch cheese, wooden clogs, or Dutch licorice.

For a more bohemian, artsy vibe, head to Noordermarkt in the Jordaan district, where you can browse vintage clothing, handmade crafts, and organic products. The market is also home to one of Amsterdam's most famous flea markets, so if you're a treasure hunter, this is the place to be. You'll find everything from secondhand books and records to retro clothing and one-of-a-kind home décor items.

3. The Flower Market (Bloemenmarkt)

No trip to Amsterdam is complete without visiting the world-famous Bloemenmarkt—the only floating flower market in the world. While it's mostly known for its colorful displays of tulips, the market is also a great place to pick up souvenirs like flower bulbs, traditional Dutch wooden clogs, and handcrafted gifts. The market's floating stalls sit along the Singel Canal, making for a scenic shopping experience that's quintessentially Amsterdam.

Guide to Local Crafts and Dutch Design

Amsterdam is a hub for creative talent, and its shops are brimming with locally crafted products that reflect the country's artistic spirit. Dutch design is known for its innovative use of simple forms, clean lines, and a unique blend of functionality and beauty. From furniture and home décor to fashion and art, Dutch craftsmanship is showcased in many shops across the city.

1. Dutch Design Shops: Innovation Meets Style

If you're drawn to minimalistic and cutting-edge design, you'll find plenty to admire in Amsterdam's design stores. Stedelijk Museum Shop, located next to the renowned Stedelijk Museum of modern art, offers a curated collection of Dutch design items, including stylish furniture, home accessories, and books on art and design. You can also check out Puik Art, a concept store that showcases the best in contemporary Dutch design. Here, you'll find unique pieces ranging from home décor to wearable art, all crafted by up-and-coming local designers.

Another must-visit for design lovers is Droog, a gallery and store that exemplifies Dutch innovation in design. With its bold and playful approach, Droog features everything from furniture and lighting to small home accessories, all reflecting a sense of fun and creativity that is uniquely Dutch.

2. Handcrafted Dutch Goods

For those interested in buying truly authentic and handmade Dutch products, Amsterdam is full of stores that sell locally crafted goods. Van Wees in the city center offers artisanal Dutch leather bags, wallets, and belts, each hand-crafted with exceptional care and quality. Similarly, Clogs and Wood specializes in traditional Dutch wooden clogs—both decorative and functional—and offers a variety of custom designs.

For a more contemporary take on Dutch craftsmanship, Kunst & Vrienden in the Jordaan showcases a range of locally made ceramics, jewelry, and textiles. It's the perfect place to pick up a beautifully crafted souvenir that represents the artistic heritage of the Netherlands.

Best Spots for Vintage Treasures

Amsterdam is a city where old meets new, and nowhere is this more evident than in its thriving vintage scene. If you're on the hunt for a unique, pre-loved item, Amsterdam is brimming with fantastic vintage shops and secondhand markets where you can find everything from retro clothing and antique furniture to vinyl records and vintage cameras.

1. Vintage Shopping in the Jordaan District

The Jordaan, known for its picturesque canals and cobbled streets, is also home to some of the best vintage shops in the city. One of the most popular spots is Episode, a vintage store known for its curated selection of secondhand clothes and accessories. Whether you're looking for a vintage leather jacket or a quirky graphic tee, Episode has something for every style. Another great shop in the area is Zipper, a well-loved store that offers a wide range of pre-loved clothing from different eras. It's an essential stop for anyone interested in fashion from the past.

2. The IJ-Hallen Flea Market

If you're in the mood for treasure hunting, make sure to check out IJ-Hallen, one of Europe's largest and most famous flea markets. Located in Amsterdam-Noord, IJ-Hallen takes place every month and features over 750 stalls selling everything from vintage clothing and furniture to antiques and collectibles. It's the perfect place to find a unique piece of Amsterdam history—whether it's a 1970s lamp, an old Dutch postcard, or a vintage vinyl album.

3. Vintage Furniture and Antiques

For vintage furniture and home décor, Amsterdam offers some hidden gems. The Retro Store in the De Pijp district is a popular spot for mid-century modern furniture, lighting, and home accessories. Similarly, Kroonenberg Antiques in the heart of the city is the place to go if you're searching for antique Dutch pieces, from classic Delftware to vintage art and furniture. Many of these shops offer one-of-a-kind pieces that make for a truly memorable souvenir, especially if you're looking to bring a slice of Dutch history into your home.

Shopping Tips for Souvenirs

When it comes to souvenirs, Amsterdam has something for everyone, from traditional Dutch clogs and cheese to artisanal crafts and contemporary design. But the best way to shop is by venturing off the beaten path and exploring some of the lesser-known spots. Whether you're shopping for a gift for a loved one or a special keepsake for yourself, Amsterdam's unique shops and markets are sure to provide a memorable experience. Here are a few tips to make your shopping experience even better:

Buy Local: Look for products that are locally made, whether it's Dutch cheese, handmade ceramics, or Dutch-designed fashion.

Explore the Markets: Amsterdam's markets offer great deals on everything from fresh produce to antiques, so don't be afraid to haggle a bit or pick up a quirky find.

Look for Limited Editions: Many shops in Amsterdam sell limited-edition or artisanal items that you won't find anywhere else, so keep an eye out for something truly unique.

Nightlife and Entertainment

Amsterdam's nightlife is as diverse and dynamic as the city itself. From bustling dance floors in world-renowned nightclubs to intimate bars serving cocktails, live music venues, and one-of-a-kind experiences like night canal cruises, the city transforms as the sun sets, offering something for every kind of night owl. Whether you're looking to dance until dawn, enjoy an elegant cocktail in a cozy bar, or immerse yourself in local culture through theater and performance, Amsterdam's nightlife promises unforgettable memories.

Amsterdam's Nightlife Scene
Clubs, Bars, and Live Music

Amsterdam is known for its vibrant and eclectic nightlife scene that appeals to people of all tastes and interests. The city offers an impressive range of options, from lively nightclubs and hip bars to intimate music venues, all with a distinct Amsterdam twist.

1. Iconic Nightclubs for Party Lovers

Amsterdam's clubbing scene is internationally recognized, with some of the best electronic music venues in the world. The city's nightlife attracts party-goers from all corners of the globe, and its nightclubs are famed for hosting world-class DJs and unforgettable parties.

De School – One of the city's most iconic venues, De School is a multi-functional space housed in a former school building. This underground nightclub features incredible acoustics and a relaxed, industrial vibe. Famous for its all-night dance parties, it's the go-to place for lovers of techno, house, and experimental beats.

Shelter – A staple of Amsterdam's nightlife scene, Shelter offers high-energy dance floors and a top-notch sound system. Known for its minimalistic design and focus on electronic music, the club hosts both local and international DJs, creating an atmosphere of inclusivity and freedom.

Marktkantine – For those who appreciate a more alternative party atmosphere, Marktkantine offers an excellent mix of electronic and indie music. The venue features intimate sets with a creative and local crowd, ensuring that you'll always have a good time no matter the night.

2. Relaxed Bars and Cozy Pubs

Not all of Amsterdam's nightlife revolves around intense dancing. The city boasts plenty of bars and pubs where you can relax and enjoy a drink in a laid-back atmosphere. Amsterdam's variety of cozy brown cafés, where locals sip their beer in a relaxed, convivial environment, creates an intimate side to the city's nightlife.

The Bulldog – For a quintessential Amsterdam experience, head to The Bulldog, one of the city's first "coffeeshops" (cannabis café). This iconic spot has become a landmark, offering a space where patrons can smoke, relax, and enjoy a drink in the heart of the city.

Bar Botanique – A tropical-themed bar that oozes charm, Bar Botanique serves as a perfect place for cocktails, with its lush décor of plants, comfortable seating, and laid-back vibe. Whether you're looking to unwind with a classic cocktail or something a little more adventurous, this bar delivers.

3. Live Music Venues for Music Lovers

Amsterdam has a thriving live music scene, with venues offering everything from jazz and rock to indie and world music. Whether you're looking for a cozy setting or a grand performance hall, the city has something for all tastes.

Melkweg – This famous venue regularly hosts top-tier acts across all genres, from rock bands to pop stars and electronic DJs. Melkweg has a rich history, dating back to the 1970s, and remains one of the city's premier spots for live music, featuring performances in an intimate and high-energy setting.

Bimhuis – For jazz lovers, Bimhuis is an essential stop. Located by the water, it offers world-class jazz performances in a sleek, modern space. It's known for its unique acoustic properties and its dedication to both established and emerging jazz talent.

Paradiso – Housed in a former church, Paradiso is one of the most iconic venues in Amsterdam. It has hosted some of the biggest names in music, from David Bowie to The Rolling Stones. The venue offers a wide variety of genres, with concerts and live shows happening almost every night.

The Best Theater and Performance Venues

Amsterdam's cultural scene is rich and diverse, with a wealth of opportunities to enjoy live theater, dance, and performance art. Whether you're after a classic show, an avant-garde performance, or something in between, the city offers a broad range of venues that cater to different tastes.

1. Royal Theatre Carré

If you're looking for a traditional theatrical experience, look no further than Royal Theatre Carré, one of the most prestigious theaters in Amsterdam. Known for its beautiful architecture and outstanding acoustics, Carré hosts a variety of performances, from classical music and opera to circus shows and ballet. The grand setting and world-class productions make it an iconic cultural institution.

2. Het Concertgebouw

Music lovers should not miss a visit to Het Concertgebouw, one of the world's most famous concert halls. Located near Museumplein, it is renowned for its stunning acoustics and its eclectic range of performances, including classical concerts, jazz, and contemporary music. You can experience the Royal Concertgebouw Orchestra here, which is considered one of the finest in the world.

3. Toneelgroep Amsterdam (Theatre Company)

For contemporary theater, Toneelgroep Amsterdam is a must-see. This cutting-edge theater company stages innovative productions in various locations around the city, often pushing the boundaries of performance art. Expect modern, thought-provoking productions that tackle both Dutch and international themes with a fresh, artistic flair.

4. The National Ballet and Opera

For lovers of ballet and opera, Amsterdam's National Ballet and Opera is a world-class venue that offers performances from international artists and companies. The company performs in the beautiful National Opera & Ballet Theatre on Amstel, offering a sophisticated setting for those looking to enjoy a night of elegance and artistry.

Unique Experiences
Night Canal Cruises and More

While Amsterdam's traditional nightlife offers clubs and bars, the city also excels in unique, once-in-a-lifetime experiences that you can enjoy after dark. These special activities offer you a chance to see the city from a different perspective, combining relaxation with the opportunity to soak in Amsterdam's beauty at night.

1. Night Canal Cruises

Amsterdam's canals are perhaps the most iconic part of the city, and they take on a magical quality at night. A night canal cruise is one of the best ways to experience the city's beauty and charm after dark. Imagine floating along the illuminated canals, passing beneath romantic bridges while enjoying a drink or a dinner on board. The boats are often heated and cozy, making it a perfect option year-round. Some tours even offer special themed cruises, like dinner cruises or private boat rentals, allowing for a unique and personal experience.

2. Amsterdam's Red Light District at Night

While often a topic of controversy, the Red Light District is also a fascinating part of Amsterdam's history and culture. At night, the district comes alive with neon lights and a different kind of energy. A guided tour through the area can provide valuable insights into the history of Amsterdam's more liberal attitudes and how the district fits into the larger cultural landscape.

3. Night at the Museums

Amsterdam's famous museums, such as the Rijksmuseum and Van Gogh Museum, are not just for daytime visitors. Many of the city's cultural institutions offer special evening events, like Night at the Museum programs, where the exhibits are open late, often with live music, art installations, or themed tours. These events offer a chance to experience the city's culture in a new light.

4. Outdoor Cinemas and Film Screenings

For those looking for something a little more relaxed, check out one of Amsterdam's many outdoor cinemas or pop-up film screenings. During the summer months, Pluk de Nacht offers open-air movie nights along the water, allowing you to enjoy a film under the stars. Many theaters also offer late-night screenings of cult films or special events, perfect for film lovers who want to unwind in a more unique setting.

Sample Itineraries

Amsterdam is a city that can be explored in many different ways, whether you have just a day to spare or a few days to dive deeper into its culture, history, and vibrant neighborhoods. Below are three sample itineraries designed to help you make the most of your time in this extraordinary city. Whether you're looking for a quick whirlwind tour, a long weekend getaway, or a family-friendly itinerary, these plans will guide you to the must-see sights while giving you a taste of what makes Amsterdam so special.

Amsterdam in 24 Hours
Making the Most of a Day

If you only have one day to explore Amsterdam, don't worry—while it's impossible to see everything, you can still pack in many of the city's highlights in just 24 hours. Here's a suggested itinerary that covers some of the top attractions, along with some hidden gems to give you a complete Amsterdam experience.

Morning:

- **Start at the Rijksmuseum:** Begin your day at the world-renowned Rijksmuseum, one of the most iconic museums in the world. The museum opens early, so get there right when it opens to beat the crowds. Spend an hour or two soaking in Dutch masterpieces from artists like Rembrandt, Vermeer, and Frans Hals. Don't miss

Rembrandt's The Night Watch, one of the most famous paintings in the world.

- **Stroll Through Vondelpark:** After the museum, head outside and take a relaxing stroll through Vondelpark, Amsterdam's largest and most famous park. It's a perfect spot for a morning walk, surrounded by beautiful greenery, ponds, and charming cafes. Stop for a coffee at one of the park's outdoor cafes and people-watch as locals start their day.

Midday:

- **Canal Cruise:** No visit to Amsterdam is complete without a cruise along the city's UNESCO-listed canals. Hop on a boat at Damrak and embark on a scenic canal tour. During the ride, you'll get a unique perspective of the city, passing beneath picturesque bridges and by colorful canal houses. Some boats even offer a lunch option, allowing you to enjoy the sights while munching on traditional Dutch snacks.

- **Lunch at a Local Café:** After the cruise, grab a bite to eat at one of Amsterdam's charming cafes. The Pancake Bakery on Prinsengracht is a great choice for a traditional Dutch pancake, or you can head to the Café de Klos for a taste of the Netherlands' famous ribs.

Afternoon:

- **Visit the Anne Frank House:** Spend the afternoon immersing yourself in one of Amsterdam's most important historical sites: the Anne Frank House. This emotional experience will take you through the secret annex where Anne Frank and her family hid during World War II. It's a sobering and poignant experience, offering a deeper understanding of Amsterdam's wartime history.

- **Explore the Jordaan District:** Once you've visited the Anne Frank House, take a walk through the Jordaan District, one of Amsterdam's most picturesque neighborhoods. Wander through its narrow streets lined with independent boutiques, art galleries, and cozy cafés. This area also has several hidden courtyards and canals, making it perfect for an afternoon stroll.

Evening:

- **Dinner at a Trendy Restaurant:** For dinner, head to De Pijp, one of Amsterdam's most vibrant neighborhoods, where you'll find a mix of global cuisines. The Avocado Show offers creative dishes centered around—you guessed it—avocados. If you're in the mood for classic Dutch food, Moeders is the place to go for comforting, hearty meals.

- **End with Drinks at a Rooftop Bar:** After dinner, end your day at one of Amsterdam's rooftop bars, such as A'DAM Lookout, where you can enjoy panoramic views of the city. If you're looking for something more intimate, SkyLounge offers a chic, relaxed atmosphere where you can sip cocktails while watching the sunset over the canals.

Three Days in Amsterdam
A Perfect Long Weekend

If you have three days to explore Amsterdam, you can take a more leisurely approach and explore the city's neighborhoods, museums, and hidden gems. This itinerary balances sightseeing with time to relax and soak in the city's atmosphere.

Day 1: The Essential Amsterdam Experience

- **Morning: Rijksmuseum and Van Gogh Museum:** Start your first full day with a visit to two of Amsterdam's must-see museums: the Rijksmuseum and the Van Gogh Museum. While the Rijksmuseum is packed with Dutch art from the Golden Age, the Van Gogh Museum offers a deep dive into the life and works of the legendary painter. Expect to spend at least two hours at each museum.

- **Lunch at Museumplein:** After your museum tour, enjoy lunch at one of the cafés in Museumplein. Café Loetje is known for its delicious steak sandwiches, while Rijks offers a more refined dining experience with views of the museum gardens.

- **Afternoon: Stroll through the Vondelpark and Canal Tour:** After lunch, take a relaxing walk through Vondelpark, and enjoy the greenery and outdoor art installations. Then, hop on a canal boat for an hour-long tour through Amsterdam's iconic waterways.

- **Evening: Dinner at the Jordaan:** Head to the Jordaan District for dinner at a cozy restaurant. Brouwerij 't IJ, a local brewery, serves hearty dishes paired with their own craft beers, while Cafe de Klos is a beloved spot for smoked meats.

Day 2: Hidden Gems and Local Culture

- **Morning: The Anne Frank House and Westerkerk:** Begin the day at the Anne Frank House, followed by a visit to the nearby Westerkerk (Western Church). The church's tower offers stunning views of the city and is a peaceful place to reflect after your Anne Frank visit.

- **Lunch in De Pijp:** For lunch, head to the lively De Pijp district. Visit the famous Albert Cuyp Market to sample Dutch street foods like stroopwafels and herring or try something international at the many cafes and eateries around the area.

- **Afternoon: Explore the Red Light District and the Hidden Courtyards:** Spend the afternoon walking through the Red Light District, where you'll find more than just its notorious reputation. Explore some of the quaint courtyards and visit The Hash Marihuana & Hemp Museum to learn about Amsterdam's marijuana culture.

- **Evening: Dinner and Drinks at the NDSM Wharf:** In the evening, take a ferry to Amsterdam-Noord to visit the NDSM Wharf, an industrial area now home to artists and creative spaces. The NDSM werf has an array of restaurants and bars where you can enjoy dinner and drinks by the water.

Day 3: A Day of Leisure and Local Flavor

- **Morning: A Visit to the Bloemenmarkt and the Heineken Experience:** Start your final day with a trip to the Bloemenmarkt, Amsterdam's floating flower market. Browse the vibrant stalls selling fresh flowers and souvenirs. Afterward, head to the Heineken Experience, an interactive museum about the famous Dutch beer.

- **Lunch at a Local Café:** Enjoy lunch at a traditional Dutch café, such as De Koffieschenkerij in the Jordaan or Café Winkel 43, known for its delicious apple pie.

- **Afternoon: Walk through Amsterdam-Noord and the A'DAM Lookout:** For the afternoon, take a trip to

Amsterdam-Noord, which offers both creative spaces and natural beauty. Don't miss the A'DAM Lookout for a breathtaking view of Amsterdam from the top of the tower.

- **Evening: Dinner and Live Music:** End your trip with dinner at one of Amsterdam's top restaurants. For live music, head to Paradiso, a legendary venue that hosts a variety of musical acts. Afterward, enjoy a nightcap at one of Amsterdam's rooftop bars to take in your last view of this beautiful city.

Family-Friendly Itinerary
Fun for Kids and Adults Alike

Amsterdam is a fantastic destination for families, offering a variety of attractions that are fun for kids and adults alike. This itinerary includes both cultural experiences and family-friendly activities, making it perfect for a multi-generational trip.

Day 1: Cultural and Fun Exploration

- **Morning: NEMO Science Museum:** Begin your family adventure with a visit to the NEMO Science Museum, one of the best interactive science museums in the world. It's hands-on and engaging for kids of all ages. They'll love exploring the exhibits and taking part in experiments that demonstrate science in a fun and accessible way.
- **Lunch at the Museum Café:** After a morning of learning, grab lunch at the NEMO Science Museum's café. It offers a variety of snacks and light meals that are perfect for recharging before the next activity.

- **Afternoon: Vondelpark and the Playground:** Head to Vondelpark, where the whole family can relax. The park features several playgrounds, a skate park, and even a pond with swan boats. It's a great place for a family picnic or a leisurely stroll.
- **Evening: Dinner at a Family-Friendly Restaurant:** Finish the day with a casual dinner at The Pancake Bakery, where kids can choose from a variety of sweet and savory pancakes, and the whole family can enjoy a relaxed meal.

Day 2: Amusement and Adventure

- **Morning: Artis Zoo:** Visit Artis Zoo, Amsterdam's oldest zoo, for a fun and educational experience. The zoo is home to a variety of animals, including giraffes, lions, and dolphins. There's also a planetarium and an aquarium, making it a perfect spot for both fun and learning.

- **Lunch at the Zoo Café:** Enjoy lunch at Artis Zoo's café, where you can refuel before continuing your exploration of the zoo.

- **Afternoon: Canal Cruise and Ice Cream:** In the afternoon, take the family on a canal cruise to experience Amsterdam from the water. It's a relaxing way to see the city and its beautiful canals, and kids will love the chance to spot the various houseboats along the way.

- **Evening: Dinner and Fun at the NDSM Wharf:** For dinner, head to the NDSM

Wharf, where there are family-friendly dining options, along with plenty of open space for kids to run around. It's a perfect way to end your day, with the chance to explore some creative, artistic spaces while enjoying a relaxed evening with your family.

Day Trips from Amsterdam

While Amsterdam offers a wealth of attractions and experiences, there's a whole world waiting just outside the city. Whether you want to immerse yourself in traditional Dutch heritage, wander through charming towns, or visit scenic canals, the Netherlands is brimming with fascinating destinations just a short train or bus ride from the city.

Zaanse Schans

Windmills and Dutch Heritage

One of the most iconic images of the Netherlands is the sight of picturesque windmills scattered across the countryside, and Zaanse Schans offers a chance to step back in time and experience this traditional Dutch landscape. Located just a 30-minute train ride from Amsterdam, Zaanse Schans is a historic village that showcases Dutch culture and craftsmanship at its finest.

The Windmills

The highlight of Zaanse Schans is undoubtedly its collection of well-preserved windmills. These iconic structures once served as functional factories, grinding grain, sawing wood, and producing oil. Today, you can step inside some of the windmills and learn about their history and the role they played in Dutch industry. The De Kat Windmill, for example, still produces paint pigments using traditional methods.

Traditional Dutch Crafts

In addition to the windmills, Zaanse Schans is home to several museums and workshops that highlight traditional Dutch craftsmanship. You can visit the Zaanse Schans Museum, which offers an interactive experience that walks you through the history of the area. Be sure to stop by the Cheese Factory, where you can sample some of the finest Dutch cheeses, or the Wooden Shoe Workshop, where you can watch artisans carve out classic wooden clogs.

Charming Scenery

The village itself is a living museum, with wooden houses dating back to the 18th and 19th centuries. Strolling through Zaanse Schans is like walking through a postcard of traditional Dutch life. The vibrant green of the fields, the scent of fresh hay, and the constant whirring of the windmill blades create a truly authentic Dutch experience.

Zaanse Schans offers the perfect blend of heritage, culture, and beautiful scenery—making it a must-visit day trip from Amsterdam.

Haarlem

A Charming Escape

Just a short 15-minute train ride from Amsterdam, Haarlem offers a perfect escape from the hustle and bustle of the city. Known for its beautiful historic architecture, cobbled streets, and a laid-back atmosphere, Haarlem is often referred to as the "city of flowers" due to its proximity to the famous tulip fields. However, this charming town has much more to offer than just its natural beauty.

Historic Attractions

Haarlem is steeped in history, and a stroll through its cobbled streets will quickly immerse you in its old-world charm. The Grote Markt (Great Market Square) is the heart of Haarlem, lined with stunning buildings like the St. Bavo's Church, a towering Gothic structure that houses a magnificent organ once played by Mozart. The church is one of the most beautiful in the Netherlands, with a tranquil atmosphere that invites you to explore its grand interior.

Museum of the History of Haarlem

For those interested in local history, the Teylers Museum is a must-visit. It's the oldest museum in the Netherlands, founded in the 18th century, and boasts an impressive collection of scientific instruments, fossils, and art. The museum is housed in an elegant 18th-century building, giving visitors a glimpse into Haarlem's intellectual past.

Boutiques and Cafés

Haarlem is also known for its vibrant shopping scene, particularly when it comes to local boutiques. Explore the narrow streets lined with unique shops, art galleries, and stylish cafés. Stop for a coffee at Café de Vijfhoek, a cozy café known for its delicious pastries and warm atmosphere.

A Visit to the Tulip Fields

If you're visiting in spring, make sure to take a short trip to the Keukenhof Gardens, just outside Haarlem. The gardens are a celebration of the Netherlands' iconic tulip fields, where you'll find acres of colorful blooms, creating a perfect scene for a springtime photo op.

Haarlem offers a quiet yet culturally rich alternative to Amsterdam, making it a perfect day trip for those seeking a mix of history, charm, and scenic beauty.

Giethoorn
The "Venice of the North"

Known as the "Venice of the North," Giethoorn is a fairy-tale village that offers one of the most unique experiences in the Netherlands. Located about an hour and a half northeast of Amsterdam, Giethoorn is a car-free village where the primary mode of transport is by boat. With its thatched-roof cottages, tranquil canals, and lush greenery, it feels like stepping into a different world.

Canal Tours

The best way to explore Giethoorn is by boat. You can rent a small boat and cruise through the peaceful canals that snake through the village. The boat ride offers a view of charming cottages and peaceful gardens, with nothing but the sounds of water and birds in the air. For an even more magical experience, consider a guided boat tour to learn about the village's history and its unique water-based transportation system.

Walking and Cycling

If you prefer to stay on land, Giethoorn also has an extensive network of walking and cycling paths that allow you to explore its picturesque surroundings. The village is surrounded by lush greenery and nature reserves, making it a great spot for birdwatching or simply enjoying the peaceful atmosphere.

Traditional Dutch Architecture

Giethoorn is famous for its well-preserved traditional Dutch architecture. The thatched-roof cottages are straight out of a storybook, and many of the homes are adorned with beautiful flower boxes in the warmer months. As you wander the village, you'll notice the lovely bridges that cross over the canals, adding to the charm of this peaceful village.

Visit the Giethoorn Museum

For those interested in learning more about the history of the village, the Giethoorn Museum offers fascinating exhibits on how the village came to be, its connection to the water, and the history of the region's peat bogs. The museum is a wonderful addition to a day trip, providing context and deeper insights into the village's way of life.

A day trip to Giethoorn feels like stepping into a timeless paradise, where nature and history intertwine seamlessly, making it one of the most peaceful and unique day trips from Amsterdam.

Volendam and Edam
Cheese, Canals, and Charm

For a truly Dutch experience, head to the charming fishing towns of Volendam and Edam, located just 30 minutes from Amsterdam by bus. These two picturesque villages offer a glimpse into traditional

Dutch life, with canals, cheese markets, and colorful wooden houses. Volendam is known for its vibrant atmosphere, while Edam exudes a quieter, more intimate charm.

Volendam: A Traditional Fishing Village

Volendam is one of the most visited villages in the Netherlands, and for good reason. This quaint town has retained its old-world charm with its iconic wooden houses and traditional fishing boats. Take a stroll along the harbor, where you can watch local fishermen at work, or explore the cobbled streets lined with shops and restaurants. Volendam is also famous for its traditional Dutch costumes, and you'll often see locals dressed in their distinctive attire, offering an excellent photo opportunity.

Cheese in Edam

Just a short drive from Volendam is Edam, home to the world-famous Edam cheese. The town is known for its picturesque canals, cobbled streets, and the iconic Edam Cheese Market. Visit one of the local cheese shops to sample the famous cheese, or stop by the Edam Cheese Museum to learn more about the production process and history of Dutch cheese-making.

Historic Attractions in Edam

Edam also boasts several historic sites, including the Edam Church, which dates back to the 15th century, and the Edams Museum, which offers insights into the town's rich history as a trading hub for cheese. The town is a tranquil place to spend the afternoon, with lovely shops and cafés offering a chance to relax and soak up the charming atmosphere.

Scenic Canals and Polders

Both Volendam and Edam are surrounded by the scenic beauty of the Dutch polders—lands that have been reclaimed from the sea and are now used for farming. The flat landscape, dotted with canals and windmills, is perfect for cycling or walking. Renting a bike and exploring the surrounding countryside offers a truly authentic Dutch experience.

A day trip to Volendam and Edam offers a delightful mix of culture, history, and natural beauty. From cheese markets and fishing villages to scenic canals and traditional Dutch architecture, this is the perfect way to experience the heart of rural Holland just a short trip from Amsterdam.

Practical Tips and Resources

Traveling to a new city can sometimes feel overwhelming, especially when you're visiting a vibrant and bustling destination like Amsterdam. But don't worry—whether you're preparing for your trip or already exploring the canals, this section is packed with practical tips and resources to ensure your Amsterdam adventure goes off without a hitch.

Packing Essentials for Amsterdam

Amsterdam is a city that combines history, culture, and modern convenience, and the weather can vary quite a bit throughout the year. Packing smartly will help ensure that you stay comfortable while enjoying everything this amazing city has to offer.

Weather Considerations

The weather in Amsterdam can be unpredictable, especially during the spring and fall months. It's always a good idea to pack layers, as temperatures can fluctuate throughout the day. Make sure to bring a light jacket or a waterproof coat—rain is common year-round, so you'll want to stay dry while you explore. In winter, temperatures can dip, so packing a warm coat and scarf is essential. Summer days are usually mild, but packing comfortable, breathable clothing and sunscreen will keep you comfortable in the sun.

Comfortable Footwear

Amsterdam is a city best explored on foot or by bike, so be sure to pack comfortable walking shoes.

You'll be doing a lot of walking along cobbled streets and canal-side paths, so opt for shoes that are durable and comfortable for all-day wear. If you plan on cycling, bike-friendly shoes are a plus, especially for those who want to cycle like a local.

Daypack or Small Backpack

A small backpack or a crossbody bag will be handy for carrying essentials like water, snacks, a map, and any items you pick up along the way. This is especially useful if you plan to explore museums or take a canal cruise, where you might want to keep your hands free.

Electronics and Adapters

Amsterdam uses 220V power outlets, and the plug type is C or F, so make sure to bring the appropriate adapter if you're coming from abroad. Don't forget your phone charger, portable power bank, and camera—you'll want to capture the beautiful canals, historical landmarks, and picturesque streets!

Health and Hygiene Items

While Amsterdam is a modern, well-equipped city, it's always helpful to carry a few personal hygiene items like tissues, hand sanitizer, and any prescription medications you might need. For extra comfort, bring along a refillable water bottle—Amsterdam's tap water is some of the cleanest in the world, so you can easily refill it throughout the day.

Essential Dutch Phrases for Tourists

While English is widely spoken throughout Amsterdam, learning a few key Dutch phrases can go a long way in enhancing your experience. It's always appreciated when visitors make an effort to speak the local language, and you might even find it opens up some interesting conversations. Here are a few phrases that will come in handy:

Greetings and Polite Phrases

- Hallo (Hello)
- Goedemorgen (Good morning)
- Goedenavond (Good evening)
- Dag (Goodbye)
- Alstublieft (Please)
- Dank u wel (Thank you)
- Excuseer me (Excuse me)
- Spreekt u Engels? (Do you speak English?)

Common Questions

- Hoe gaat het? (How are you?)
- Waar is de dichtstbijzijnde tramhalte? (Where is the nearest tram stop?)
- Hoeveel kost dit? (How much is this?)
- Kunt u me helpen? (Can you help me?)
- Waar is het toilet? (Where is the bathroom?)

Getting Around

- Links (Left)
- Rechts (Right)
- Rechtdoor (Straight ahead)
- Stapt u hier uit? (Do I get off here?)

While English is common in tourist areas, these simple phrases can help you connect with locals and enhance your experience. Don't be afraid to ask for help or strike up a conversation—Amsterdam's residents are known for being friendly and approachable.

Emergency Contacts and Safety Tips

Amsterdam is generally a very safe city for tourists, but like any major destination, it's always smart to take precautions and be prepared. Here are some essential emergency contacts and safety tips to keep in mind:

Emergency Numbers

- **112:** Emergency services (police, ambulance, fire)
- **0900-8844:** Non-emergency police assistance
- GGD Amsterdam: Public health services (for medical issues not requiring immediate attention)
- Local pharmacies: You can find pharmacies throughout the city, and many are open 24 hours. Look for the **"Apotheek"** sign.

Safety Tips

- **Pickpocketing:** While Amsterdam is generally safe, it's always a good idea to be cautious of pickpockets, especially in crowded places like markets, trams, and tourist attractions. Keep your valuables in a secure bag, and avoid displaying expensive items like jewelry or cameras in busy areas.

- **Cycling Safety:** Amsterdam is known for its bike-friendly infrastructure, but biking in the city can be hectic for first-time riders. Always check for cyclists before crossing bike lanes, and be aware of your surroundings. If you plan to rent a bike, wear a helmet for extra safety.
- **Street Smarts:** Like any major city, be aware of your surroundings, especially in less crowded areas or after dark. Stick to well-lit streets, avoid alleyways at night, and be mindful of your belongings.

If you ever find yourself in need of assistance, don't hesitate to approach a local or contact the nearest police station. The city's residents are often more than willing to lend a helping hand.

Insider Hacks to Save Money and Time

Amsterdam can be an expensive city, especially when you're indulging in its world-class museums, trendy dining spots, and picturesque canal tours. But there are plenty of ways to save money and make the most of your visit without compromising on the experience. Here are some insider tips to help you stretch your budget further:

Use the I Amsterdam City Card

The I Amsterdam City Card is an absolute must-have for visitors planning to see multiple attractions. It offers free or discounted entry to top museums, including the Rijksmuseum, Van Gogh Museum, and Stedelijk Museum, as well as free use of public transport, including trams, buses, and boats. If you're staying for a few days and plan on visiting several museums and attractions, the card can save you a lot of money and time.

Explore by Bike

Biking is the best way to get around Amsterdam—both for convenience and cost. Many local rental shops offer affordable bike rentals, and cycling is a great way to explore the city like a local. It's fast, eco-friendly, and often quicker than navigating the trams or buses, especially during rush hour.

Free Activities

Amsterdam has plenty of free activities that are just as enjoyable as any paid attraction. Spend a day in Vondelpark, the city's largest park, perfect for a picnic or leisurely walk. The Begijnhof is another peaceful spot where you can relax and soak in the city's historic charm, free of charge. Also, keep an eye out for free festivals or events, especially during the summer months.

Eat Like a Local

While Amsterdam has an excellent dining scene, it's easy to spend a lot on meals in tourist-heavy areas. Instead, venture to local neighborhoods like De Pijp or Jordaan, where you'll find affordable yet delicious eateries serving up everything from Indonesian rijsttafel to fresh herring. Don't forget to grab a quick, budget-friendly snack at one of the city's street markets, where you can sample local favorites like stroopwafels or poffertjes (mini pancakes).

Book Tickets in Advance

For major attractions, it's always a good idea to book tickets online in advance. Not only will you often get a discount, but you'll also skip long queues, saving you valuable time. Many museums and tours also offer time slots, so you can plan your day efficiently and avoid the crowds.

Conclusion

As your journey through the canals, museums, and vibrant neighborhoods of Amsterdam comes to a close, one thing becomes clear: this city is far more than just a place to visit; it's a place to feel, to experience, and to connect with. Whether you've strolled along the famous canal-side paths, marveled at world-renowned art, or simply lost yourself in the charm of a quiet café, Amsterdam leaves an indelible mark on all who wander through its streets.

Amsterdam is a city of contrasts—a place where history and modernity coexist harmoniously. It's where you can sip a coffee in a 17th-century café while checking the latest tech news on your phone. It's where the artistic genius of Van Gogh mingles with the bold creativity of its contemporary designers. It's a city that invites you to slow down, savor the moment, and, at the same time, offers endless opportunities for discovery and excitement.

In this guide, we've shared not just the must-see attractions, but also the little-known gems that make Amsterdam truly special. From iconic museums to peaceful parks, from the vibrant nightlife to the serene beauty of its waterways, Amsterdam offers something for every traveler. The beauty of this city isn't just in its picturesque architecture or its world-class art scene; it's in the spirit of the people, the culture, and the welcoming atmosphere that wraps around you as you explore.

As you plan your own Amsterdam adventure, remember that this city is one you can come back to again and again. With each visit, you'll uncover new layers, new experiences, and new memories. Whether you're here for a short weekend getaway or an extended stay, Amsterdam promises a fresh perspective on every corner.

So, what are you waiting for? Your adventure in this dynamic, fascinating city is ready to unfold. From wandering along the iconic canals to discovering hidden treasures in its neighborhoods, the best of Amsterdam is waiting for you to dive in.

Make the most of your time, embrace the local culture, and, most importantly, let Amsterdam's charm and beauty sweep you off your feet. This city is more than just a destination—it's an experience that will stay with you long after you've left its cobbled streets behind.

See you in Amsterdam! Your adventure is just beginning.

Printed in Great Britain
by Amazon